Key Facts™ on Yemen

~Essential Information on Yemen~

By Patrick W. Nee

The Internationalist®
www.internationalist.com

The Internationalist®

International Business, Investment, and Travel

Published by:

The Internationalist Publishing Company

96 Walter Street/ Suite 200

Boston, MA 02131, USA

Tel: 617-354-7722

www.internationalist.com

PN@internationalist.com

Copyright © 2013 by PWN

The Internationalist is a Registered Trademark. "Key Facts" and "The Internationalist Business Guides" are Trademarks of The Internationalist Publishing Company.

All Rights are reserved under International, Pan-American, and Pan-Asian Conventions. No part of this book may be reproduced in any form without the written permission of the publisher. All rights vigorously enforced

Table Of Contents

Chapter 1: Background

Chapter 2: Geography

Chapter 3: People and Society

Chapter 4: Government and Key Leaders

Chapter 5: Economy

Chapter 6: Energy

Chapter 7: Communications

Chapter 8: Transportation

Chapter 9: Military

Chapter 10: Transnational Issues

Map of Yemen

Chapter 1: Background

North Yemen became independent of the Ottoman Empire in 1918. The British, who had set up a protectorate area around the southern port of Aden in the 19th century, withdrew in 1967 from what became South Yemen. Three years later, the southern government adopted a Marxist orientation. The massive exodus of hundreds of thousands of Yemenis from the south to the north contributed to two decades of hostility between the states. The two countries were formally unified as the Republic of Yemen in 1990. A southern secessionist movement and brief civil war in 1994 was quickly subdued. In 2000, Saudi Arabia and Yemen agreed to a delimitation of their border. Fighting in the northwest between the government and Huthi rebels, a group seeking a return to traditional Zaydi Islam, began in 2004 and has since resulted in six rounds of fighting - the last ended in early 2010 with a cease-fire that continues to hold. The southern secessionist movement was revitalized in 2008 when a popular socioeconomic protest movement initiated the prior year took on political goals including secession. Public rallies in Sana'a against then President SALIH - inspired by similar demonstrations in Tunisia and Egypt - slowly built momentum starting in late January 2011 fueled by complaints over high unemployment, poor economic conditions, and corruption. By the following month, some protests had resulted in violence, and the demonstrations had spread to other major cities. By March the opposition had hardened its demands and was unifying behind calls for SALIH's immediate ouster. The Gulf Cooperation Council (GCC) in late April 2011, in an attempt to mediate the crisis in Yemen, proposed an agreement in which the president would step down in exchange for immunity from prosecution. SALIH's refusal to sign an agreement led to heavy street fighting and his injury in an explosion in June 2011. The UN Security Council passed Resolution 2014 in October 2011 calling on both sides to end the violence and complete a power transfer deal. In late November 2011, SALIH signed the GCC-brokered agreement to step down and to transfer some of his powers to Vice President Abd Rabuh Mansur HADI. Following elections in February 2012, won by HADI, SALIH formally transferred his powers. In accordance with the GCC initiative, Yemen launched a National Dialogue to discuss key constitutional, political, and social issues in mid-March 2013.

Chapter 2: Geography

Location:

Middle East, bordering the Arabian Sea, Gulf of Aden, and Red Sea, between Oman and Saudi Arabia

Geographic coordinates:

15 00 N, 48 00 E

Map references:

Middle East

Area:

total: 527,968 sq km

country comparison to the world: 50

land: 527,968 sq km

water: 0 sq km

note: includes Perim, Socotra, the former Yemen Arab Republic (YAR or North Yemen), and the former People's Democratic Republic of Yemen (PDRY or South Yemen)

Area - comparative:

slightly larger than twice the size of Wyoming

Land boundaries:

total: 1,746 km

border countries: Oman 288 km, Saudi Arabia 1,458 km

Coastline:

1,906 km

Maritime claims:

territorial sea: 12 nm

contiguous zone: 24 nm

exclusive economic zone: 200 nm

continental shelf: 200 nm or to the edge of the continental margin

Climate:

mostly desert; hot and humid along west coast; temperate in western mountains affected by seasonal monsoon; extraordinarily hot, dry, harsh desert in east

Terrain:
>narrow coastal plain backed by flat-topped hills and rugged mountains; dissected upland desert plains in center slope into the desert interior of the Arabian Peninsula

Elevation extremes:
>lowest point: Arabian Sea 0 m
>
>highest point: Jabal an Nabi Shu'ayb 3,760 m

Natural resources:
>petroleum, fish, rock salt, marble; small deposits of coal, gold, lead, nickel, and copper; fertile soil in west

Land use:
>arable land: 2.2%
>
>permanent crops: 0.55%
>
>other: 97.25% (2011)

Irrigated land:
>6,801 sq km (2004)

Total renewable water resources:
>2.1 cu km (2011)

Freshwater withdrawal (domestic/industrial/agricultural):
>total: 3.57 cu km/yr (7%/2%/91%)
>
>per capita: 162.4 cu m/yr (2005)

Natural hazards:
>sandstorms and dust storms in summer
>
>volcanism: limited volcanic activity; Jebel at Tair (Jabal al-Tair, Jebel Teir, Jabal al-Tayr, Jazirat at-Tair) (elev. 244 m), which forms an island in the Red Sea, erupted in 2007 after awakening from dormancy; other historically active volcanoes include Harra of Arhab, Harras of Dhamar, Harra es-Sawad, and Jebel Zubair, although many of these have not erupted in over a century

Environment - current issues:
>limited natural freshwater resources; inadequate supplies of potable water; overgrazing; soil erosion; desertification

Environment - international agreements:

    party to: Biodiversity, Climate Change, Climate Change-Kyoto Protocol, Desertification, Endangered Species, Environmental Modification, Hazardous Wastes, Law of the Sea, Ozone Layer Protection
    signed, but not ratified: none of the selected agreements

Geography - note:
    strategic location on Bab el Mandeb, the strait linking the Red Sea and the Gulf of Aden, one of world's most active shipping lanes

Chapter 3: People and Society

Nationality:
    noun: Yemeni(s)
    adjective: Yemeni

Ethnic groups:
    predominantly Arab; but also Afro-Arab, South Asians, Europeans

Languages:
    Arabic (official)

Religions:
    Muslim (Islam - official) including Shaf'i (Sunni) and Zaydi (Shia), small numbers of Jewish, Christian, and Hindu

Population:
    25,408,288 (July 2013 est.)
    country comparison to the world: 47

Age structure:
    0-14 years: 42% (male 5,433,121/female 5,235,891)
    15-24 years: 21.1% (male 2,720,793/female 2,640,652)
    25-54 years: 30.6% (male 3,974,091/female 3,797,543)
    55-64 years: 3.7% (male 446,293/female 490,628)
    65 years and over: 2.6% (male 315,141/female 354,135) (2013 est.)

Median age:
    total: 18.5 years
    male: 18.4 years
    female: 18.6 years (2013 est.)

Population growth rate:
    2.5% (2013 est.)
    country comparison to the world: 30

Birth rate:
    31.63 births/1,000 population (2013 est.)
    country comparison to the world: 38

Death rate:

    6.64 deaths/1,000 population (2013 est.)

    country comparison to the world: 145

Net migration rate:

    0 migrant(s)/1,000 population (2013 est.)

    country comparison to the world: 80

Urbanization:

    urban population: 32.3% of total population (2011)

    rate of urbanization: 4.78% annual rate of change (2010-15 est.)

Major urban areas - population:

    SANAA (capital) 2.229 million (2009)

Sex ratio:

    at birth: 1.05 male(s)/female

    0-14 years: 1.04 male(s)/female

    15-24 years: 1.03 male(s)/female

    25-54 years: 1.05 male(s)/female

    55-64 years: 0.92 male(s)/female

    65 years and over: 0.9 male(s)/female

    total population: 1.03 male(s)/female (2013 est.)

Maternal mortality rate:

    200 deaths/100,000 live births (2010)

    country comparison to the world: 56

Infant mortality rate:

    total: 51.93 deaths/1,000 live births

    country comparison to the world: 38

    male: 56.33 deaths/1,000 live births

    female: 47.31 deaths/1,000 live births (2013 est.)

Life expectancy at birth:

    total population: 64.47 years

    country comparison to the world: 175

    male: 62.39 years

female: 66.65 years (2013 est.)

Total fertility rate:

    4.27 children born/woman (2013 est.)

    country comparison to the world: 34

Contraceptive prevalence rate:

    27.7% (2006)

Health expenditures:

    5.2% of GDP (2010)

    country comparison to the world: 132

Physicians density:

    0.3 physicians/1,000 population (2009)

Hospital bed density:

    0.7 beds/1,000 population (2010)

Drinking water source:

    improved:

        urban: 72% of population

        rural: 47% of population

        total: 55% of population

    unimproved:

        urban: 28% of population

        rural: 53% of population

        total: 45% of population (2010 est.)

Sanitation facility access:

    improved:

        urban: 93% of population

        rural: 34% of population

        total: 53% of population

    unimproved:

        urban: 7% of population

        rural: 66% of population

        total: 47% of population (2010 est.)

HIV/AIDS - adult prevalence rate:

0.1% (2001 est.)

country comparison to the world: 139

HIV/AIDS - people living with HIV/AIDS:

12,000 (2001 est.)

country comparison to the world: 91

HIV/AIDS - deaths:

NA

Major infectious diseases:

degree of risk: high

food or waterborne diseases: bacterial diarrhea, hepatitis A, and typhoid fever

vectorborne diseases: dengue fever and malaria

water contact disease: schistosomiasis (2013)

Obesity - adult prevalence rate:

14.5% (2008)

country comparison to the world: 121

Children under the age of 5 years underweight:

43.1% (2003)

country comparison to the world: 3

Education expenditures:

5.2% of GDP (2008)

country comparison to the world: 65

Literacy:

definition: age 15 and over can read and write

total population: 63.9%

male: 81.2%

female: 46.8% (2010 est.)

School life expectancy (primary to tertiary education):

total: 9 years

male: 11 years

female: 7 years (2005)

Child labor - children ages 5-14:
    total number: 1,334,288

    percentage: 23 % (2006 est.)

Mother's mean age at first birth:
    19.2

    note: Median age at first birth among women 25-29 (1997 est.)

Chapter 4: Government and Key Leaders

Country name:
    conventional long form: Republic of Yemen
    conventional short form: Yemen
    local long form: Al Jumhuriyah al Yamaniyah
    local short form: Al Yaman
    former: Yemen Arab Republic [Yemen (Sanaa) or North Yemen] and People's Democratic Republic of Yemen [Yemen (Aden) or South Yemen]

Government type:
    republic

Capital:
    name: Sanaa
    geographic coordinates: 15 21 N, 44 12 E
    time difference: UTC+3 (8 hours ahead of Washington, DC during Standard Time)

Administrative divisions:
    20 governorates (muhafazat, singular - muhafazah) and 1 municipality*; Abyan, 'Adan (Aden), Ad Dali', Al Bayda', Al Hudaydah, Al Jawf, Al Mahrah, Al Mahwit, Amanat al 'Asimah (Sanaa City)*, 'Amran, Dhamar, Hadramawt, Hajjah, Ibb, Lahij, Ma'rib, Raymah, Sa'dah, San'a' (Sanaa), Shabwah, Ta'izz

Independence:
    22 May 1990 (Republic of Yemen was established with the merger of the Yemen Arab Republic [Yemen (Sanaa) or North Yemen] and the Marxist-dominated People's Democratic Republic of Yemen [Yemen (Aden) or South Yemen]); note - previously North Yemen became independent in November 1918 (from the Ottoman Empire) and became a republic with the overthrow of the theocratic Imamate in 1962; South Yemen became independent on 30 November 1967 (from the UK)

National holiday:
    Unification Day, 22 May (1990)

Constitution:
    16 May 1991; amended 29 September 1994 and February 2001

Legal system:
> mixed legal system of Islamic law, Napoleonic law, English common law, and customary law

International law organization participation:
> has not submitted an ICJ jurisdiction declaration; non-party state to the ICCt

Suffrage:
> 18 years of age; universal

Executive branch:
> <u>chief of state</u>: President Abd Rabuh Mansur HADI (Field Marshal) (since 25 February 2012)
>
> <u>head of government</u>: Prime Minister Muhammad Salim BA SINDWAH (since 27 November 2011)
>
> <u>cabinet</u>: on 27 November 2011, Vice President HADI requested Interim Prime Minister Muhammad Salim BA SINDWAH to form a new government following the resignation of President SALIH on 24 November 2011
>
> <u>elections</u>: president elected by popular vote for a seven-year term based on constitution; however a special election was held on 21 February 2012 to remove Ali Abdallah SALIH based on a GCC-mediated deal during the political crisis of 2011 (next election to be held in 2014); vice president appointed by the president but position is vacant; prime minister appointed by the president
>
> <u>election results</u>: Abd Rabuh Mansur HADI elected as a consensus president with about 50% popular participation; no other candidates

Legislative branch:
> bicameral legislature consisting of a Shura Council (111 seats; members appointed by the president) and House of Representatives (301 seats; members elected by popular vote in single-member constituencies to serve six-year terms)
>
> <u>elections</u>: last held on 27 April 2003 (scheduled April 2009 election postponed)
>
> <u>election results</u>: House of Representatives percent of vote by party - NA; seats by party - GPC 238, Islah 47, YSP 6, Nasserite Unionist Party 3, National Arab Socialist Ba'th Party 2, independents 5

Judicial branch:

highest court(s): Supreme Court (consists of the president of the Court, 2 deputies, and nearly 50 judges; court organized into constitutional, civil, commercial, family, administrative, criminal, military, and appeals scrutiny divisions)

judge selection and term of office: judges appointed by the Supreme Judicial Council, chaired by the president of the republic and consisting of 10 high-ranking judicial officers; judges appointed for life with mandatory retirement at age 65

subordinate courts: appeal courts; district or first instance courts; commercial courts

Political parties and leaders:

General People's Congress or GPC [Ali Abdallah SALIH, Abd Rabuh Mansur HADI]

Islamic Reform Grouping or Islah [Muhammed Abdallah al-YADUMI, Abdul Wahab al-ANSI]

Nasserite Unionist Party [Sultan al-ATWANI]

Yemeni Socialist Party or YSP [Yasin Said NU'MAN]

note: there are at least seven more active political parties

Political pressure groups and leaders:

Muslim Brotherhood

Women National Committee

other: conservative tribal groups; Huthis, southern secessionist groups; al-Qa'ida in the Arabian Peninsula (AQAP)

International organization participation:

AFESD, AMF, CAEU, CD, EITI (compliant country), FAO, G-77, IAEA, IBRD, ICAO, ICRM, IDA, IDB, IFAD, IFC, IFRCS, ILO, IMF, IMO, IMSO, Interpol, IOC, IOM, IPU, ISO, ITSO, ITU, ITUC (NGOs), LAS, MIGA, MINURSO, MONUSCO, NAM, OAS (observer), OIC, OPCW, UN, UNAMID, UNCTAD, UNESCO, UNHCR, UNIDO, UNISFA, UNMIL, UNMIS, UNOCI, UNWTO, UPU, WCO, WFTU (NGOs), WHO, WIPO, WMO, WTO (observer)

Diplomatic representation in the US:

chief of mission: Ambassador (vacant); Charge d'Affaires Adel Ali Ahmed AL-SUNAINI

chancery: 2319 Wyoming Avenue NW, Washington, DC 20008

telephone: [1] (202) 965-4760

FAX: [1] (202) 337-2017

Diplomatic representation from the US:

chief of mission: Ambassador Gerald M. FEIERSTEIN

embassy: Sa'awan Street, Sanaa

mailing address: P. O. Box 22347, Sanaa

telephone: [967] (1) 755-2000 ext. 2153 or 2266

FAX: [967] (1) 303-182

Key Leaders:

Pres.	**Abd Rabuh Mansur HADI**, *Fd. Mar.*
Prime Min.	**Muhammad Salim BA SINDWAH**
Min. of Agriculture & Irrigation	**Farid Ahmad MUJAWWAR**
Min. of Civil Service & Social Security	**Nabil Abduh SHAMSAN**
Min. of Communications & Information Technology	**Ahmad Ubayd BIN DAGHIR**
Min. of Culture	**Abdallah Awabil MANTHUQ**
Min. of Defense	**Muhammad Nasir Ahmad ALI**, *Maj. Gen.*
Min. of Education	**Abd al-Razaq al-ASHWAL**
Min. of Electricity & Energy	**Salih Hasan SUMIYA**
Min. of Expatriate Affairs	**Mujahid al-QAHALI**
Min. of Finance	**Sakhir Ahmad Abbas al-WAJIH**

Min. of Fisheries	**Awadh al-SUQUTRI**
Min. of Foreign Affairs	**Abu Bakr Abdallah al-QIRBI**
Min. of Higher Education & Scientific Research	**Hisham Sharaf ABDALLAH**
Min. of Human Rights	**Huriya Ahmad MASHHUR**
Min. of Industry & Trade	**Saad al-Din Ali Salim bin TALIB**
Min. of Information	**Ali Ahmad Muhammad al-AMRANI**
Min. of Interior	**Abd al-Qadir QAHTAN,** *Maj. Gen.*
Min. of Justice	**Murshid al-ARSHANI**
Min. of Legal Affairs	**Muhammad Ahmad al-MIKHLAFI**
Min. of Local Admin.	**Ali al-YAZIDI**
Min. of Oil & Minerals	**Ahmad Abdallah DARIS**
Min. of Planning & Intl. Cooperation	**Muhammad al-SAADI**
Min. of Public Health & Population	**Ahmad Qasim al-ANISI,** *Dr.*
Min. of Public Works & Roads	**Umar Abdallah al-KARASHMI**
Min. of Religious Endowment & Islamic Affairs	**Hamud Muhammad ABAD**
Min. of Social Affairs & Labor	**Amat al-Razaq Ali HAMAD**

Min. of Technical Education & Vocational Training	Abd al-Hafiz NU'MAN
Min. of Tourism	Abduh al-JANADI
Min. of Transport	Wa'id Abdullah BA THIB
Min. of Water & Environment	Abd al-Salaam RAZAZ
Min. of Youth & Sports	Mu'ammar al-IRYANI
Min. of State	Shayif Azi SAGHIR
Min. of State for Cabinet Affairs	Jawhara Hamud THABIT
Min. of State & Dir. of Prime Min.'s Office	Muhammad ZAFIR
Min. of State & Mayor of Sanaa	Abd al-Rahman Muhammad AL-AKWA
Min. of State for Parliamentary & Shura Council Affairs	Rashad Ahmad al-RASAS
Governor, Central Bank	Muhammad Awadh Ali bin HUMAM
Ambassador to the US	
Permanent Representative to the UN, New York	Jamal Abdallah al-SALLAL

Flag description:

three equal horizontal bands of red (top), white, and black; the band colors derive from the Arab Liberation flag and represent oppression (black), overcome through bloody struggle (red), to be replaced by a bright future (white) note: similar to the flag of Syria, which has two green stars in the white band, and of Iraq, which has an Arabic inscription centered in the white band; also similar to the flag of Egypt, which has a heraldic eagle centered in the white band

National symbol(s):
golden eagle

National anthem:
name: "al-qumhuriyatu l-muttahida" (United Republic)
lyrics/music: Abdullah Abdulwahab NOA'MAN/Ayyoab Tarish ABSI
note: adopted 1990; the music first served as the anthem for South Yemen before unification with North Yemen in 1990

Chapter 5: Economy

Economy - overview:

Yemen is a low income country that is highly dependent on declining oil resources for revenue. Petroleum accounts for roughly 25% of GDP and 70% of government revenue. Yemen has tried to counter the effects of its declining oil resources by diversifying its economy through an economic reform program initiated in 2006 that is designed to bolster non-oil sectors of the economy and foreign investment. In October 2009, Yemen exported its first liquefied natural gas as part of this diversification effort. In January 2010, the international community established the Friends of Yemen group that aims to support Yemen's efforts toward economic and political reform. In 2012, the Friends of Yemen pledged over $7 billion in assistance to Yemen. The Yemeni government also endorsed a Mutual Accountability Framework to facilitate the efficient implementation of donor aid. The unrest that began in early 2011 caused GDP to plunge more than 15% in 2011, and about 2%in 2012. Availability of basic services, including electricity, water, and fuel, has improved since the transition, but progress toward achieving more sustainable economic stability has been slow and uneven. Yemen continues to face difficult long term challenges, including declining water resources, high unemployment, and a high population growth rate.

GDP (purchasing power parity):

$60.06 billion (2012 est.)

country comparison to the world: 89

$59.97 billion (2011 est.)

$66.99 billion (2010 est.)

note: data are in 2012 US dollars

GDP (official exchange rate):

$35.64 billion (2012 est.)

GDP - real growth rate:

0.1% (2012 est.)

country comparison to the world: 177

-10.5% (2011 est.)

7.7% (2010 est.)

GDP - per capita (PPP):

$2,300 (2012 est.)

country comparison to the world: 188

$2,400 (2011 est.)

$2,700 (2010 est.)

note: data are in 2012 US dollars

GDP - composition by sector:

agriculture: 8.5%

industry: 36%

services: 55.5% (2012 est.)

Labor force:

7.158 million (2012 est.)

country comparison to the world: 63

Labor force - by occupation:

note: most people are employed in agriculture and herding; services, construction, industry, and commerce account for less than one-fourth of the labor force

Unemployment rate:

35% (2003 est.)

country comparison to the world: 184

Population below poverty line:

45.2% (2003)

Household income or consumption by percentage share:

lowest 10%: 2.9%

highest 10%: 30.8% (2005)

Distribution of family income - Gini index:

37.7 (2005)

country comparison to the world: 74

33.4 (1998)

Investment (gross fixed):

18% of GDP (2012 est.)

country comparison to the world: 116

Budget:
>revenues: $7.359 billion
>
>expenditures: $11.2 billion (2012 est.)

Taxes and other revenues:
>20.6% of GDP (2012 est.)
>
>country comparison to the world: 160

Budget surplus (+) or deficit (-):
>-10.8% of GDP (2012 est.)
>
>country comparison to the world: 207

Public debt:
>43% of GDP (2012 est.)
>
>country comparison to the world: 82
>
>36.5% of GDP (2011 est.)

Inflation rate (consumer prices):
>10.2% (2012 est.)
>
>country comparison to the world: 200
>
>19.5% (2011 est.)

Central bank discount rate:
>NA%

Commercial bank prime lending rate:
>23% (31 December 2012 est.)
>
>country comparison to the world: 12
>
>25% (31 December 2011 est.)

Stock of narrow money:
>$5.142 billion (31 December 2012 est.)
>
>country comparison to the world: 99
>
>$4.645 billion (31 December 2011 est.)

Stock of broad money:
>$10.59 billion (31 December 2012 est.)
>
>country comparison to the world: 105

$10.17 billion (31 December 2011 est.)
Stock of domestic credit:
$9.576 billion (31 December 2012 est.)
country comparison to the world: 101
$7.662 billion (31 December 2011 est.)
Market value of publicly traded shares:
$NA
Agriculture - products:
grain, fruits, vegetables, pulses, qat, coffee, cotton; dairy products, livestock (sheep, goats, cattle, camels), poultry; fish
Industries:
crude oil production and petroleum refining; small-scale production of cotton textiles and leather goods; food processing; handicrafts; small aluminum products factory; cement; commercial ship repair; natural gas production
Industrial production growth rate:
0.8% (2012 est.)
country comparison to the world: 123
Current account balance:
-$2.19 billion (2012 est.)
country comparison to the world: 139
-$1.663 billion (2011 est.)
Exports:
$7.604 billion (2012 est.)
country comparison to the world: 103
$8.662 billion (2011 est.)
Exports - commodities:
crude oil, coffee, dried and salted fish, liquefied natural gas
Exports - partners:
China 37.3%, Thailand 15.8%, South Korea 11.4%, India 9.9%, UAE 5.3% (2012)
Imports:
$8.893 billion (2012 est.)

country comparison to the world: 100
$8.248 billion (2011 est.)

Imports - commodities:
food and live animals, machinery and equipment, chemicals

Imports - partners:
China 15.7%, UAE 14.4%, India 9.7%, Saudi Arabia 6.8%, Kuwait 5.1% (2012)

Reserves of foreign exchange and gold:
$6.158 billion (31 December 2012 est.)
country comparison to the world: 85
$4.531 billion (31 December 2011 est.)

Debt - external:
$7.395 billion (31 December 2012 est.)
country comparison to the world: 108
$6.418 billion (31 December 2011 est.)

Stock of direct foreign investment - at home:
$NA

Exchange rates:
Yemeni rials (YER) per US dollar:
214.35 (2012 est.)
213.8 (2011 est.)
219.59 (2010 est.)
202.85 (2009)
199.76 (2008)

Fiscal year:
calendar year

Chapter 6: Energy

Electricity - production:
>6.339 billion kWh (2009 est.)
>
>country comparison to the world: 110

Electricity - consumption:
>4.7 billion kWh (2009 est.)
>
>country comparison to the world: 116

Electricity - exports:
>0 kWh (2010 est.)
>
>country comparison to the world: 151

Electricity - imports:
>0 kWh (2010 est.)
>
>country comparison to the world: 151

Electricity - installed generating capacity:
>1.33 million kW (2009 est.)
>
>country comparison to the world: 116

Electricity - from fossil fuels:
>100% of total installed capacity (2009 est.)
>
>country comparison to the world: 2

Electricity - from nuclear fuels:
>0% of total installed capacity (2009 est.)
>
>country comparison to the world: 207

Electricity - from hydroelectric plants:
>0% of total installed capacity (2009 est.)
>
>country comparison to the world: 153

Electricity - from other renewable sources:
>0% of total installed capacity (2009 est.)
>
>country comparison to the world: 207

Crude oil - production:
>162,100 bbl/day (2011 est.)

country comparison to the world: 44

Crude oil - exports:

191,100 bbl/day (2009 est.)

country comparison to the world: 31

Crude oil - imports:

0 bbl/day (2009 est.)

country comparison to the world: 145

Crude oil - proved reserves:

2.88 billion bbl (1 January 2013 est.)

country comparison to the world: 31

Refined petroleum products - production:

83,130 bbl/day (2008 est.)

country comparison to the world: 79

Refined petroleum products - consumption:

177,000 bbl/day (2011 est.)

country comparison to the world: 61

Refined petroleum products - exports:

18,140 bbl/day (2008 est.)

country comparison to the world: 74

Refined petroleum products - imports:

61,950 bbl/day (2008 est.)

country comparison to the world: 61

Natural gas - production:

6.24 billion cu m (2010 est.)

country comparison to the world: 51

Natural gas - consumption:

760 million cu m (2010 est.)

country comparison to the world: 95

Natural gas - exports:

5.48 billion cu m (2010 est.)

country comparison to the world: 29

Natural gas - imports:

0 cu m (2010 est.)

country comparison to the world: 82

Natural gas - proved reserves:

478.5 billion cu m (1 January 2012 est.)

country comparison to the world: 33

Carbon dioxide emissions from consumption of energy:

26.5 million Mt (2010 est.)

country comparison to the world: 78

Chapter 7: Communications

Telephones - main lines in use:

1.075 million (2011)

country comparison to the world: 74

Telephones - mobile cellular:

11.668 million (2011)

country comparison to the world: 68

Telephone system:

general assessment: since unification in 1990, efforts have been made to create a national telecommunications network

domestic: the national network consists of microwave radio relay, cable, tropospheric scatter, GSM and CDMA mobile-cellular telephone systems; fixed-line and mobile-cellular teledensity remains low by regional standards

international: country code - 967; landing point for the international submarine cable Fiber-Optic Link Around the Globe (FLAG); satellite earth stations - 3 Intelsat (2 Indian Ocean and 1 Atlantic Ocean), 1 Intersputnik (Atlantic Ocean region), and 2 Arabsat; microwave radio relay to Saudi Arabia and Djibouti (2006)

Broadcast media:

state-run TV with 2 stations; state-run radio with 2 national radio stations and 5 local stations; stations from Oman and Saudi Arabia can be accessed (2007)

Internet country code:

.ye

Internet hosts:

33,206 (2012)

country comparison to the world: 105

Internet users:

2.349 million (2009)

country comparison to the world: 71

Chapter 8: Transportation

Airports:

    57 (2012)

    country comparison to the world: 84

Airports - with paved runways:

    total: 17

    over 3,047 m: 4

    2,438 to 3,047 m: 9

    1,524 to 2,437 m: 3

    914 to 1,523 m: 1 (2012)

Airports - with unpaved runways:

    total: 40

    over 3,047 m: 3

    2,438 to 3,047 m: 5

    1,524 to 2,437 m: 7

    914 to 1,523 m: 16

    under 914 m: 9 (2012)

Pipelines:

    gas 641 km; liquid petroleum gas 22 km; oil 1,370 km (2013)

Roadways:

    total: 71,300 km

    country comparison to the world: 65

    paved: 6,200 km

    unpaved: 65,100 km (2005)

Merchant marine:

    total: 5

    country comparison to the world: 126

    by type: chemical tanker 2, petroleum tanker 2, roll on/roll off 1

    registered in other countries: 14 (Moldova 4, Panama 4, Sierra Leone 2, Togo 1, unknown 3) (2010)

Ports and terminals:
    Aden, Al Hudaydah, Al Mukalla

Transportation - note:
    the International Maritime Bureau reports offshore waters in the Gulf of Aden are high risk for piracy; numerous vessels, including commercial shipping and pleasure craft, have been attacked and hijacked both at anchor and while underway; crew, passengers, and cargo are held for ransom; the presence of several naval task forces in the Gulf of Aden and additional anti-piracy measures on the part of ship operators reduced the incidence of piracy in that body of water by more than half in 2010

Chapter 9: Military

Military branches:

Land Forces, Naval and Coastal Defense Forces (includes Marines), Air and Air Defense Force (al-Quwwat al-Jawwiya al-Yemeniya), Border Guards, Stategic Reserve Forces (2013)

Military service age and obligation:

18 is the legal minimum age for voluntary military service; no conscription; 2-year service obligation (2012)

Manpower available for military service:

males age 16-49: 5,652,256

females age 16-49: 5,387,160 (2010 est.)

Manpower fit for military service:

males age 16-49: 4,056,944

females age 16-49: 4,116,895 (2010 est.)

Manpower reaching militarily significant age annually:

male: 287,141

female: 277,612 (2010 est.)

Military expenditures:

6.6% of GDP (2006)

country comparison to the world: 8

Military - note:

a Coast Guard was established in 2002

Chapter 10: Transnational Issues

Disputes - international:
>Saudi Arabia has reinforced its concrete-filled security barrier along sections of the fully demarcated border with Yemen to stem illegal cross-border activities

Refugees and internally displaced persons:
>refugees (country of origin): 4,686 (Ethiopia) (2011); 229,447 (Somalia) (2013)
>
>IDPs: at least 431,000 (conflict in Sa'ada governorate; clashes between AQAP and government forces) (2012)

Map of Yemen

Other Key Facts™ Titles

Key Facts on Syria

Key Facts on China

Key Facts on Qatar

Key Facts on India

Key Facts on Germany

Key Facts on Argentina

Key Facts on Russia

Key Facts on North Korea

Key Facts on Brazil

Key Facts on Italy

Key Facts on the United Arab Emirates

Key Facts on the European Union

Key Facts on Pakistan

Key Facts on Saudi Arabia

Key Facts on Cyprus

Key Facts on Iran

Key Facts on Afghanistan

Key Facts on Iraq

Key Facts on Indonesia

Key Facts on South Korea

Key Facts on France

Key Facts on the United Kingdom

Key Facts on Egypt
Key Facts on Israel
Key Facts on Mexico
Key Facts on the United States of America
Key Facts on Turkey
Key Facts on South Africa
Key Facts on Greece
Key Facts on Japan
Key Facts on Malaysia
Key Facts on Vietnam
Key Facts on Hong Kong
Key Facts on Jordan
Key Facts on Australia
Key Facts on Venezuela
Key Facts on Canada
Key Facts on Burma (Myanmar)
Key Facts on Myanmar (Burma)
Key Facts on Singapore
Key Facts on Ireland
Key Facts on The Philippines
Key Facts on Thailand

All Key Facts™ Titles are Available at www.Amazon.com

THE INTERNATIONALIST®
2013
WWW.INTERNATIONALIST.COM

www.ingramcontent.com/pod-product-compliance
Lightning Source LLC
Chambersburg PA
CBHW070725180526
45167CB00004B/1617